# BYE-BYE EARTHSUIT
## HELLO HEAVENSUIT

### DONNA ARLYNN FRISINGER

We, too, wait with eager hope for the day when
God will give us our full rights as his adopted children,
including the new bodies he has promised.
**Romans 8:23 (NLT)**

"For here is the way God loved the world. He gave his only, unique Son as a gift. So now everyone who believes in him will never perish but experience everlasting life. God did not send his Son into the world to judge and condemn the world, but to be its Savior and rescue it!"
(John 3:16-17 TPT)

*"Let the children come to me. For the Kingdom*
*of Heaven belongs to such as these."*
**Matthew 19:14**

# For Matty, Sammy, and Wiley

My amazing great-nephews who constantly renew
my own child-like faith and endless curiosity.

Written in honor of my grandma . . . Hettie Hope Bickham
and my mother . . . Dorothy Arlene (Bickham) Allen

Bunnies zig-zagged and squirrels played tag in the shadows of late afternoon. Holding tight to Nana, Hettie's lips quivered and Teddy hung his head.

Usually, the twins liked nothing better than playtime in the park. But today, they didn't feel like running or jumping. Skipping or singing. Hiding or seeking.

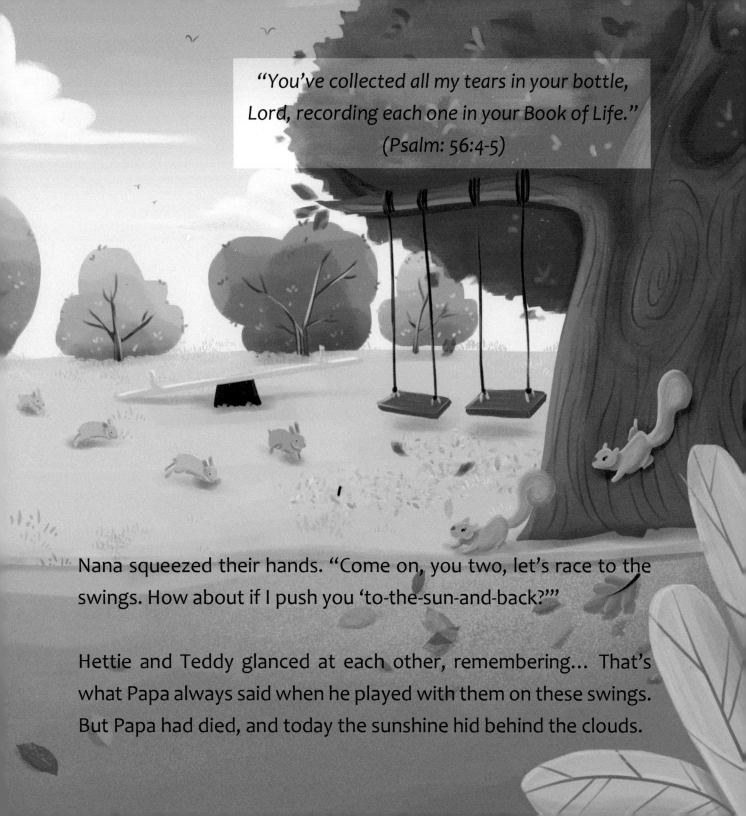

"You've collected all my tears in your bottle,
Lord, recording each one in your Book of Life."
(Psalm: 56:4-5)

Nana squeezed their hands. "Come on, you two, let's race to the swings. How about if I push you 'to-the-sun-and-back?'"

Hettie and Teddy glanced at each other, remembering... That's what Papa always said when he played with them on these swings. But Papa had died, and today the sunshine hid behind the clouds.

Back and forth, back and forth...

The swings rocked, in silence, from the old oak tree. A mourning dove cooed—counting to three: "Coo-ahh—cooo-cooo-cooo."

Nana's eyes twinkled with a memory.
She waggled her eyebrows, twiggled her nose,
and swaggled her shoulders. With a whopping-big
shove, she whooped, stooped, and swooped
beneath Teddy's swing. "Underdog!"
she called.

"Wooooah!" Teddy screeched.

"No 'Underdog' for me, please, Nana!" Hettie hiccupped.
"It makes my tummy tickle!"

"God heals the broken-hearted, and bandages their wounds."
(Psalm147:3)

Nana flopped back in the leaves, grinning. "Did you know Papa used to 'Underdog' me on these same swings years ago?"

Giggles stopped, and jaws dropped. "Really?"

*"Celebrating your rescue, I throw myself headlong into your arms, God."*
(Psalm 13:5-6)

"Yes-siree! Just like how he started playing 'Underdog' with you guys once you were old enough to walk."

Teddy jumped off the swing. "Nana, where is Papa now?"

"Yeah." Hettie dangled her feet, sniffling. "Will we ever see him again?"

Like an eagle spreading its wings, Nana lifted her arms to zoom across the grass. "Someday," she called, "we'll all leave these Earthsuits behind to get our brand-new Heavensuits."

The twins scrunched their eyes.

Nana waved for them to follow. "Come, children. Sit."

*"Those who wait upon the Lord get fresh strength*
*to spread their wings and soar like the eagles"*
(Isaiah 40:31)

Striking a pose like a fancy lady, Nana batted her eyelashes. "Ooh-la-la! What do you think of my razzle-dazzle sweater?"

Teddy squinted over his glasses. "Purple's my favorite color—"

"And the butterflies!" Hettie sighed. "I adore butterflies."

Nana raised her eyebrows. "Exactly why I've kept it all these years. Now watch."

"Open my eyes, God, to see your miracle wonders."
(Psalm 119:18)

"See how it moves? If I reach up over my head, it stretches with me. When I touch my toes, it bends over too."

TWITCHY

The twins tittered when she twisted up like a pretzel. "Why, it will even twitchy-the-twitch with me if I try to itchy-the-itch in the middle of my back."

"*A happy heart is good medicine,
and a joyful soul brings healing.*"
(Proverbs:17:22)

"But…" Nana wriggled out of the sweater. "If I toss this old thing on the ground, it can't move anymore, can it? There's no life left inside."

Teddy and Hettie stared at Nana's sweater, crumpled and rumpled in the grass.

"Would you two like to know something amazing?" Plopping down to face them, Nana continued. "The real us—the thinking, wishing, feeling part of us—is our soul. Our spirit."

Jaws dropped.

> "We can understand God's mysteries because we have the mind of Christ."
> (1 Cor.: 2:16)

She placed her hands above their hearts and whispered,
"Your spirit—the real you—lives here, inside your Earthsuits."

Teddy checked his armpits. Under his legs.
Around his back. "Are you sure, Nana?"

Nana chuckled. "The Bible tells us when life ends here on earth,
we just step out of our Earthsuits and—"

"Ugh!" Hettie gasped. "Like how you took off your purple
butterfly sweater!"

Teddy leaned closer. "Then what happens?"

"God's angels take us to a wonderful,
worry-free world." Nana closed her eyes.
"We can't see it right now.
But that place is just beyond the sun
and is as real as this park."

The twins peeked at each other. "Heaven!"

Hettie snatched up Nana's sweater and smooshed it to her cheek. It smelled like Nana—bouquets of lilacs. Her throat felt pinchy. "Will you leave your Earthsuit, too, Nana?"

*"Death is swallowed up in victory."*
(1 Cor. 15:54)

Teddy gulped. "Will we?"

Nana cuddled them into a squeezy-hug. "Sooner or later, children, every living thing comes to the end of its life. But, if we love Jesus, we go to Heaven to be with Him and all the other people who've ever loved Him."

"Like Papa?" Teddy's voice sounded crackly as he nuzzled into Nana's hug.

Nana nodded. "Like Papa. Like me. Like you, and—"

"Me!" Hettie chimed in. "I love Jesus too!"

the ducks! Splash in mud puddles! Monster Hunts!"

"Underdogs!" Teddy yelled. "Read books! Play
'Let's Go Camping!'"

*"I remember the days of old—all the good memories."*

*(Psalm 143:5)*

"We'll have us a humdinger of a party, too!" Nana twirled, raising her voice to the heavens. "Only, I won't be wearing this slow giddy-uppy, frumpy-dumpy Earthsuit anymore."

"Lordy, no. I'll be trading it for a get-up-and-go, super-duper, wrinkle-free Heavensuit. One that will never get old or sick or die."

The twins' eyes sparkled like fireworks.
"Ohhh! You mean like..."

*"We grow tired in our present bodies, and we long to put on our heavenly bodies like new clothing."*
(2 Cor. 5:2)

"Nana..." Teddy hesitated. "Do you think we could ask Jesus to give Papa a squeezy-hug from us—right now?"

"Pleeease?" Hettie pleaded.

Nana dabbed at the liquid-love leaking from the corners of her eyes. "Yes, my darlings, of course, we can."

As if on cue, the sun broke through. Sparrows hushed, the wind held its breath, and sunflowers bowed their heads.

Jesus said, "You may ask for anything in my name, and I will do it."
(John 14:14)

Teddy began:

"Dear Jesus, thank you for taking good care of Papa until we see him again in Heaven. Could you please give him a squeezy-hug from us right now?"

"And tell him we love him," Hettie added, "'to-the-sun-and-back.'" Nana squeezed their hands. "Amen."

"Death is swallowed up in victory!"
(1 Cor.15:54)

Once more, the twins soared to the tops of the trees. Clouds ran away as they sang in the breeze, "Higher, Nana, higher! 'To the sun-and-back,' higher!"

"Underdog!"

Donna Frisinger is a multi-award-winning poet and author, including a First-Place Golden Scroll Award for *Bink and Slinky's Christmas Adventure*. She and her life-long Prince Charming Barry reside in their humble castle in Indiana, where they enjoy hiking, spoiling nephews and nieces, and riding their trusty steeds (retro-look Schwinn bicycles) throughout the lay of the land.

*The passing of a loved one is not an easy topic for any age, especially children. Donna Frisinger has delivered a sweet and creative story to help children understand what happens to our bodies when we die. Her positive approach makes this a kid-friendly picture book and will serve as an excellent resource for parents, grandparents, and teachers when explaining death to children.*

## Donna's Book Awards

# MY SPECIAL MEMORIES WITH

_____

Use these pages to remember special times shared
with your loved one...

- Add photos of you together
- Draw pictures of things you did together
- Make a memory list
- Write a letter to them or to God